RSPB

RSPB first book of the seashore

Derek Niemann

A & C Black • London

Published 2012 by A&C Black, an imprint of
Bloomsbury Publishing Plc
50 Bedford Square, London, WC1B 3DP
www.acblack.com

ISBN: 978-1-4081-6569-0

Copyright © 2012 Bloomsbury Publishing Plc
Text: Derek Niemann, 2012
Illustrations: Ian Jackson, 2012

Printed and bound in China by WKT.

A&C Black uses paper produced from elemental
chlorine-free pulp, harvested from managed
sustainable forests.

Contents

The seashore

The seashore is a great place for playing
in the sand and splashing in the sea. It's
a wonderful place to see wildlife too. You
can pick up lots of shells on the beach.
But what creatures live in them? What
can you find hiding in the rock pools?

This book will help you name many of
the creatures living at the seashore. It will
tell you more about how they live and
where you might find them.

At the back of this book is a Spotter's
Guide to help you remember the things
you find at the seashore. You could also
write them down or draw pictures.

Turn the page to find out more about
seashore wildlife!

Anemone

This animal has tentacles. It catches tiny creatures in the water. If one gets too close, the anemone stings it with its tentacles. The stings don't hurt us though.

When the tide goes out, the anemone hides its tentacles in its body.

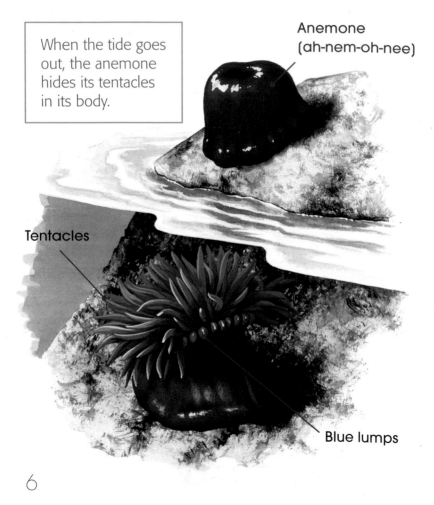

Anemone
(ah-nem-oh-nee)

Tentacles

Blue lumps

Bladder wrack

This seaweed is easy to spot. Look for its pea-sized bladders. They are filled with gas so that the seaweed can float in the water. Then it can catch the sunlight.

Look out for different kinds of seaweed. It can be brown, green or red.

Bladders

Midrib

Seaweed gets all its energy from sunlight.

The leaf is called a frond

Holdfast. This keeps the seaweed stuck to a rock

Cowrie shell

Look for these tiny shells on the beach. They have lots of ridges and a long slit down the middle that looks like a mouth. The shell belongs to an underwater snail called a cowrie.

In some countries, cowries used to be used as money.

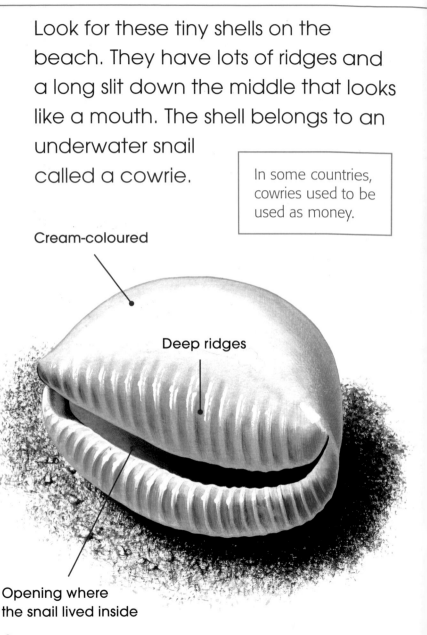

Cream-coloured

Deep ridges

Opening where the snail lived inside

Turnstone

You may see a little light and dark bird turning stones and seaweed over on the seashore. The turnstone is looking for crabs, shellfish and shrimps that live under stones.

Look out for turnstones close to the water's edge.

Dark brown and black on top

Short beak

Light underneath

9

 # Ragworm

All sorts of worms live on the shore. A ragworm swims or crawls about looking for things to eat. It has hairy bristles on the side of its body.

Watch out! The ragworm has big jaws like pincers. It usually keeps them hidden away.

Feelers

A ragworm can be as long as your hand.

Bristles

Four black eyes

Acorn barnacle

Barnacles look like tiny volcanoes. Lots of them are stuck together on the rocks. When the tide comes in, a barnacle waves its feathery legs out of the hole at the top. It catches tiny animals floating past.

Six hard pieces of shell

Feathery legs

Grey or white

Barnacles belong to the same family as crabs.

Sea slater

If you lift up a stone, you might find a sea slater. It has a very flat body, so it can squeeze into narrow spaces like a woodlouse.

The sea slater hides during the day in damp places. It comes out at night to feed on dead things.

Hard shell

Long feelers

Seven pairs of legs

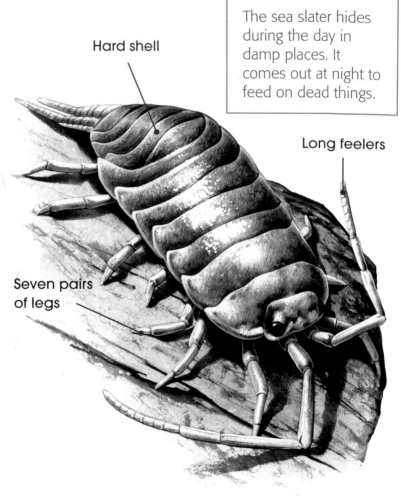

Sand hopper

What are the little
creatures jumping
about as you stand
on old seaweed?
They are sand hoppers.
Watch them spring away
on their long back legs.

Look for sand
hoppers on
the 'strandline'.
This is where
the sea washes
things up.

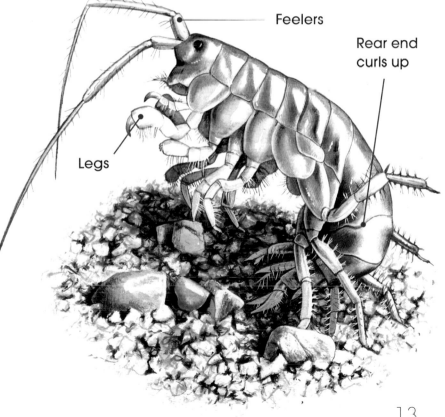

Feelers

Rear end
curls up

Legs

Common prawn

Many rockpools have prawns in them. They are almost see-through, so they are hard to spot. Watch one walking along the bottom of the pool, picking up food.

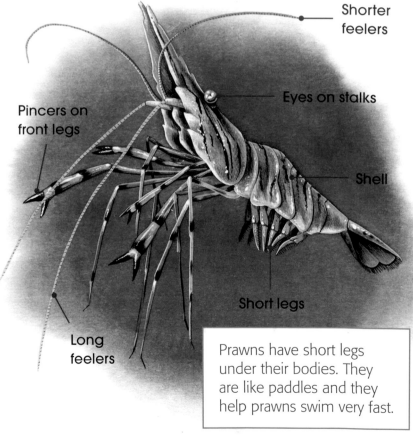

Shorter feelers

Eyes on stalks

Pincers on front legs

Shell

Short legs

Long feelers

Prawns have short legs under their bodies. They are like paddles and they help prawns swim very fast.

Shore crab

Crabs have big claws, a hard shell and little dark eyes on stalks. They hide under stones in rockpools. When they come out, they walk sideways.

When a hunter grabs a crab by the claw, the crab can let it break off. It can grow a new claw.

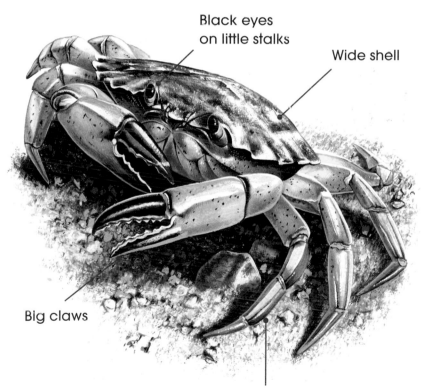

Black eyes on little stalks

Wide shell

Big claws

Legs

Hermit crab

This crab doesn't grow a shell of its own. It finds the empty shell of another creature and lives inside it. When it grows too big, it has to find a larger one.

The hermit crab walks on its front legs, pulling its home behind it.

Eyes on stalks

Shell once belonged to a whelk

The hermit crab has a soft body, so it needs a hard shell to protect it.

Big claws

Common jellyfish

This strange-looking animal has a body that looks like an umbrella. It spends most of its life floating out at sea. You may see a common jellyfish washed up on the shore.

Four circles on top

Jellyfish catch little creatures by stinging them with their tentacles.

Mouth tentacles

Stinging tentacles on edge

Some kinds of jellyfish can sting us too, so be careful!

Common limpet

When a limpet is stuck to a rock, nobody can move it! At night, or when the tide is in, it starts to move. It goes round its rock eating little plants called algae.

Limpets only ever move about a metre. They always go back to the same spot.

Hollowed out rock where limpet has been

Periwinkle

These tiny snails shelter in cracks in the rock. They come out to graze on seaweed when the tide is in. They can be dark blue, black or brightly-coloured.

Periwinkles are sometimes just called winkles.

Spiral shell

Pointed tip

Crabs eat periwinkles. So do people!

Whelk

The whelk has a tube coming out of the shell just above its head. It uses the tube to smell its prey. It drills holes into barnacle and mussel shells and eats the animal inside.

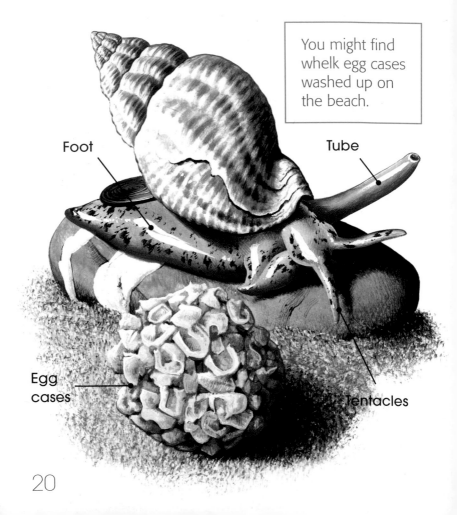

You might find whelk egg cases washed up on the beach.

Foot

Tube

Egg cases

Tentacles

Mussel

The mussel has one very strong muscle! This keeps both parts of its shell together. The mussel opens its shell a little and lets water in. Then it traps things floating in the water to eat.

Mussels keep their shells closed when they are out of water.

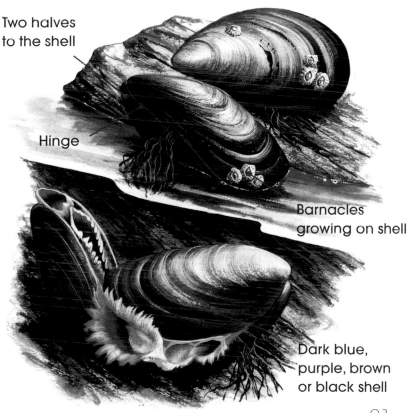

Two halves to the shell

Hinge

Barnacles growing on shell

Dark blue, purple, brown or black shell

21

Top shell

Look for top shells on the shore
near the sea. They feed on
green algae here. If you find
an empty shell, look inside.
It may be shiny and colourful.

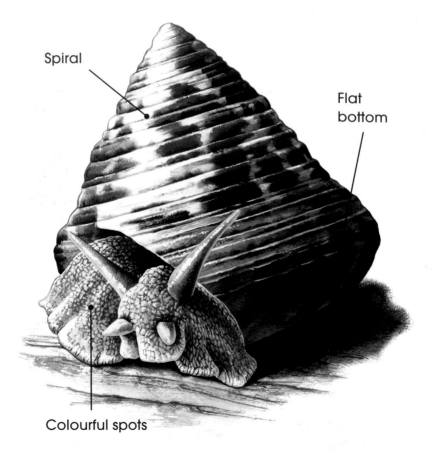

Spiral

Flat
bottom

Colourful spots

Starfish

How many arms does a starfish have? The one in the picture has five, but they can have four, five, six or seven! Starfish hunt in rockpools and on the seabed for cockles, mussels and other shellfish.

The mouth of the starfish is underneath its body.

Red or orange above

Small spines

Arm

Feet underneath for holding on

Common blenny

This rockpool fish can climb as well as swim. It uses the little fins underneath its body like arms. They help to pull it up through cracks in the rocks.

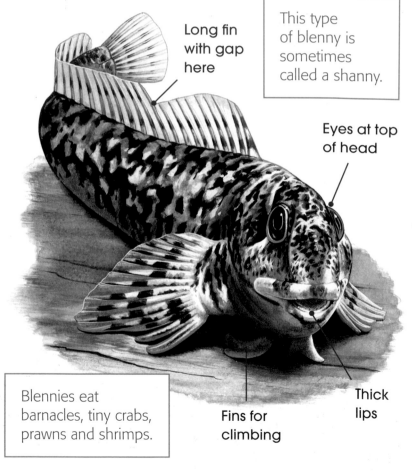

Long fin with gap here

This type of blenny is sometimes called a shanny.

Eyes at top of head

Blennies eat barnacles, tiny crabs, prawns and shrimps.

Fins for climbing

Thick lips

Grey seal

This is the seal you are most likely to see here. Sometimes you can spot its head in the water. Sometimes you see it lying on the rocks or on the beach.

Seals spend most of their lives in the sea. They catch fish to eat.

Long head

Grey seals have their babies in the autumn.

Blotchy fur

Very short flippers

Cormorant

Cormorants are long, dark birds that fly close to the water. Sometimes they stand on the shore with their wings stretched out. Nobody is quite sure why they do this.

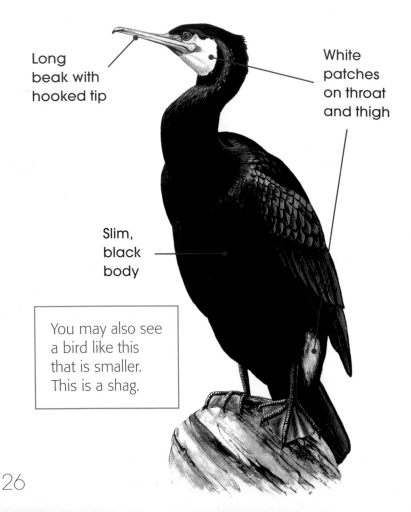

Long beak with hooked tip

White patches on throat and thigh

Slim, black body

You may also see a bird like this that is smaller. This is a shag.

Herring gull

A bird calling loudly at the seaside is probably a herring gull. It is a big, white and grey bird with a yellow beak.. You can get very close to a herring gull before it flies away.

Young herring gulls peck at the red spot on their parent's beak when they are hungry. The parent then sicks up food for them!

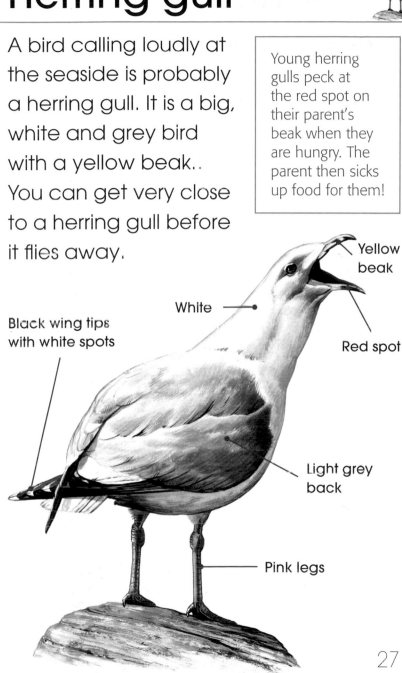

Yellow beak

White

Black wing tips with white spots

Red spot

Light grey back

Pink legs

Common goby

The goby is the same colour as the sand. It swims at the bottom of rockpools so it is very hard to spot. Look out for its little black eyes.

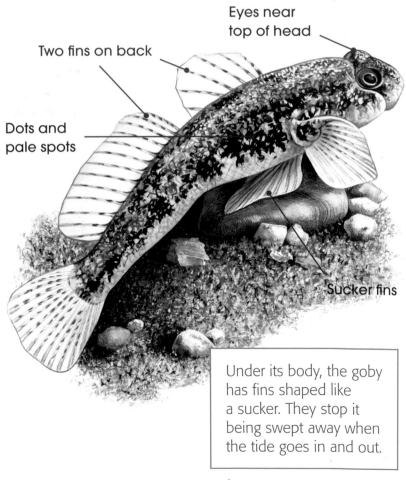

Eyes near top of head

Two fins on back

Dots and pale spots

Sucker fins

Under its body, the goby has fins shaped like a sucker. They stop it being swept away when the tide goes in and out.

Butterfish

You might think this fish
is an eel or a sea snake.
It can grow up to
25 centimetres long.

Butterfish
often hide
under stones
in rockpools.

The butterfish is a slimy, slippery fish
to hold. That's how it got its name.

Black patches with
white or yellow edge

Long fins on
back with
short spines

Long body

Small head
and mouth

# Cockle

The cockle lives in wet sand. It sucks in water through a little tube and eats tiny bits of food in the water. Then another tube squirts the water out again.

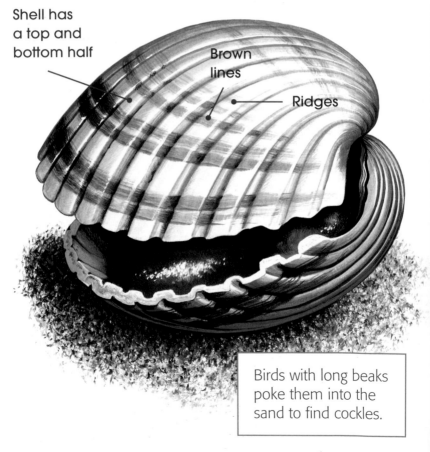

Shell has a top and bottom half

Brown lines

Ridges

Birds with long beaks poke them into the sand to find cockles.

Goose barnacle

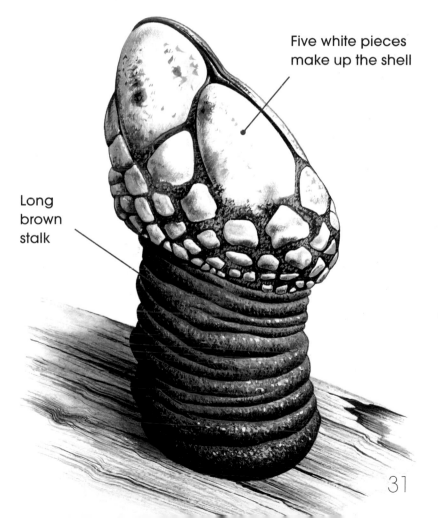

These white barnacles live far
out at sea. They often stick to a
floating piece of driftwood. Look
for them on wood that has been
washed up on the shore.

Five white pieces
make up the shell

Long
brown
stalk

Sanderling

Have you seen little birds running very fast in front of the waves? They could be sanderlings. They stop for a moment to peck up a fly or a worm.

Light underneath

Grey above. Darker in spring and summer

Short black legs

Short black beak

There are lots of other small wading birds like sanderlings that you might see on the seashore.

Oystercatcher

These black and white birds are looking for cockles and mussels to eat. They have bright red beaks and legs.

Oystercatchers make lots of loud peeping calls.

Reddish-orange beak

Red legs

# Chiton

When the tide is out, look on rocks for chitons (kye-tons). The pieces of their shell are stuck together like armour. When the tide is in, they move around the rocks, eating green algae off them.

If a chiton is washed off its rock by the sea, it rolls up into a ball.

Flat body on rock

Eight pieces make up the shell

Spines along edge

Mermaid's purse

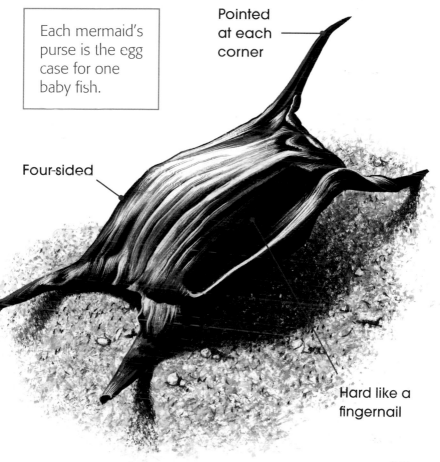

You can sometimes find these on the beach. They are old egg cases made by dogfish or other fish called rays. The fish laid their eggs in them and their babies hatched inside.

Each mermaid's purse is the egg case for one baby fish.

Pointed at each corner

Four-sided

Hard like a fingernail

 # Sponge

Sponges are animals that come in all sorts of shapes, sizes and colours. Just like the plastic sponges in your bathroom or kitchen, they soak up water through tiny holes.

Dotted surface. A sponge is full of holes.

Some sponges have names that tell you what they look like. One is called the elephant's ear.

Growing on rock

Common piddock

Look for a deep, round hole in a rock or a piece of driftwood. Maybe a piddock lived there. These animals use sharp bits on their shell to burrow into the rock. They stay there for the rest of their lives.

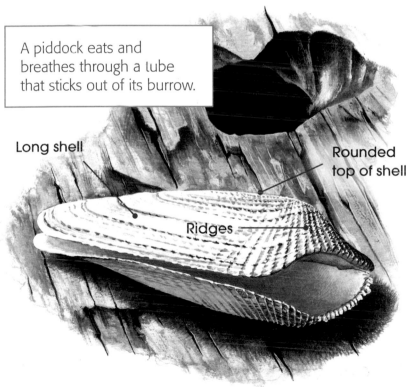

A piddock eats and breathes through a tube that sticks out of its burrow.

Long shell

Rounded top of shell

Ridges

Sea urchin

Look for a sea urchin in a rockpool. It eats seaweed. You might also find a hard, round, lumpy little ball on the beach. It is all that is left of a dead sea urchin.

The round shell is the urchin's skeleton

Lumps where spines once grew

One urchin looks like a vegetable and is called the sea potato. But you can't eat it!

Dots where sucker feet once grew

Prickly live urchin

Tubeworm

You might find thin shapes like bits of string on rocks. These hard tubes are made by this worm. It shoots out little tentacles to feed when the sea comes in.

> Some tubeworms make tubes that look like shells on seaweed.

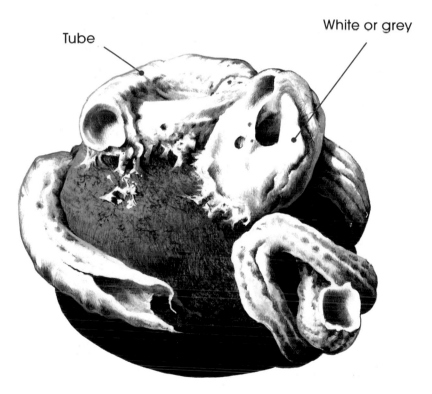

Tube

White or grey

Razorshell

Look for a very long, thin shell on the beach. It is one half of a razorshell. A creature with a soft body once lived inside.

A razorshell can burrow faster into sand than a human can dig.

Shell can be straight or curved

Razorshell burrow

Useful words

dogfish small shark that swims at the bottom of the sea

driftwood wood floating on the surface of the sea or washed up onto the beach

dunes little hills of sand at the back of the beach

pincers front claws of a prawn, crab or lobster

shellfish sea animals that usually have a shell

shingle round pebbles or small stones that make up some beaches

strandline the place on the shore where the sea washes up shells, dead plants, pieces of wood and rubbish

Spotter's guide

How many of these creatures have you seen? Tick them when you spot them.

☐ Anemone
page 6

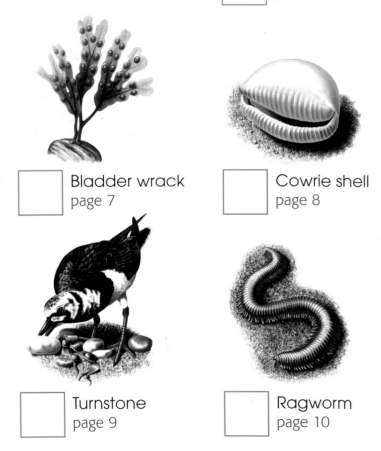

☐ Bladder wrack
page 7

☐ Cowrie shell
page 8

☐ Turnstone
page 9

☐ Ragworm
page 10

Acorn barnacle
page 11

Sea slater
page 12

Sand hopper
page 13

Common prawn
page 14

Shore crab
page 15

Hermit crab
page 16

Common jellyfish
page 17

Common limpet
page 18

Periwinkle
page 19

Whelk
page 20

Mussel
page 21

Top shell
page 22

Starfish
page 23

Common blenny
page 24

Grey seal
page 25

Cormorant
page 26

Herring gull
page 27

Common goby
page 28

Butterfish
page 29

Cockle
page 30

Goose barnacle
page 31

Sanderling
page 32

Oystercatcher
page 33

Chiton
page 34

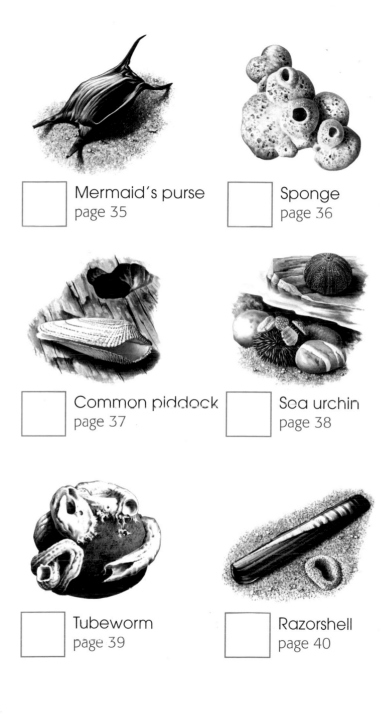

☐ Mermaid's purse
page 35

☐ Sponge
page 36

☐ Common piddock
page 37

☐ Sea urchin
page 38

☐ Tubeworm
page 39

☐ Razorshell
page 40

Find out more

If you have enjoyed this book you might like our club for children. RSPB Wildlife Explorers helps  you learn more about nature. You will get a magazine six times a year that tells you all about things you can do.

Visit the world's biggest wildlife club for children at www.rspb.org.uk/youth